God Always Hears

by Kelly Grettler

ILLUSTRATED BY SOLOMEA KALINICHENKO

God Always Hears

Printed in the USA

ISBN: 9781689776080 Paperback
ISBN: 9780578571874 Hardcover

To
Teddy Bears
&
Whispered Prayers

We got some bad news
from the Doctor today,

he said that I needed
a "Hospital Stay."

That evening,

my Mom knelt

and started to pray,

that no matter what happened,

I'd be okay.

Now praying,

in case you don't already know,

is a place

for all the bad feelings to go.

It's a way

for your sadness and uncertain tears

to be softened,

along with your worries and fears.

It may feel at first
that prayers fall on deaf ears,

but make no mistake of it,
God Always Hears.

The next day we packed

a small, leather suitcase

with my comb, and toothbrush,

and some tiny toothpaste.

I started to feel just a little bit scared

as we stuck in my blanket and slippers to wear ...

To help me feel better,

we said one more prayer,

and then, for good measure,

we packed Mr. Bear.

When we first arrived,

I thought I would cry

when the man at the desk

looked at me and said "hi."

I stood tall, took some breaths,

and tried not to be shy

as I held my mom's hand,

and then closed my eyes.

I pictured a day

with a big, bright blue sky,

and green grass,

and tall trees,

and a small butterfly.

Then we went to a room
where I sat with my Mom.

and we whispered to God
to please help me be strong.

The next thing I did

was I put on a gown,

and climbed into a bed

that could go up and down.

It had buttons, and levers,

and a hand held control,

and side rails, and four wheels,

so when pushed, it would roll.

Then a nurse, wearing frogs on her shirt, came to see me.

She explained it was time to give me an IV.

She promised that this was no cause for alarm,

then she tied a blue, tight rubber band 'round my arm.

One deep breath later, and my IV was in,

as an easier way to take medicine.

I began to feel tired,

so I let my eyes close,

when she had me

count backward from ten,

nice and slow.

I made it past eight,

then to seven or so,

and from then on I slept

and that's all that I know.

I woke up in a new place
to a new nurse's face,

this one wore a shirt
that had rockets in space.

She told me it's over,
and that I did great,

and how proud she was of me
for being so brave.

I didn't feel like talking,
and I didn't want to eat,
all I wanted to do
was go right back to sleep.
I had a strange dream
where I saw Mommy weep,
but instead heard machines
that would constantly beep.

I spent lots of days
in that hospital bed,

with white bandages wrapped
'round the top of my head.

Games were played, movies watched,

many stories were read,

along with the hundreds
of prayers that were said.

I had lots of visitors,

and those who live far,

instead sent me beautiful
flowers and cards.
Some sent balloons,

along with regards,

which helped me to smile
on the days that were hard.

Then under a glowing
rose - colored sunset,
they let me go home
after running some tests.

For the next couple weeks
Doctor said that it's best
If I stay home from school,
and I get lots of rest.

I tell myself now

that I'm strong and I'm brave

and when something new scares me,

I stop,

and I pray.

I know that whatever surprise comes my way,

no matter what happens,

I know I'm okay.

The
End.

I was inspired to write this book on the heels of a recent health scare of my own.

Not an overly religious person, I don't believe that you need to be in a church to talk to God.

Instead, I feel that He's everywhere, all around us, even when we're unable to articulate our prayers.

It was in those mind-numbing first days & early weeks of doctor visits, throughout my subsequent surgery,

and then consistently afterward as I navigated my recovery, that I found myself thinking about a lone butterfly.

Like a lot.

I think of it as a symbol of my soul, of peace, of transformation, and as a sign that God was right beside me through it all.

Because of this I was able to maintain a sense of overall courage and strength and faith.

Today, my wish for anyone who is reading this, my purpose for writing this book, is to hopefully convey that message and to attest, first hand, to the incredible power of prayer.

About the Author

Kelly Grettler lives in Cibolo, Texas
with her tolerant husband and their two amazing sons.
When she's not writing, she enjoys reading, catching up with
friends over coffee, puttering around antique shops,
and just hanging out with her family.
To find out more about Kelly,
head to www.kellygrettler.com.

ABOUT THE ILLUSTRATOR

"To reproduce the stories in the characters, to convey the characters, to tell about their lives in drawings is what I like and what I dream of connecting my life with."

-Solomea Kalinichenko

You are holding a book that is evidence of a great miracle.

One evening, my mom and I were dreaming about the future and about my profession. I asked her if I would really be able to become an illustrator and Mom told me "I believe in you incredibly." The next evening I received a message from Kelly Grettler, asking if I would be interested in illustrating this book.

The title of this book & this proposal was, for me, the answer to my question to God.

I know 100% that God Always Hears.

MY NAME IS SOLOMEA KALINICHENKO

I'm 12 years old.

I live with my mother in a small town near Kiev (Ukraine).

I study at the 4th year of art school.

I have two pets: my dog, Cassie and a rabbit, Fos.

(By the way, my dog came to me also after a big dream and prayer:

I was dreaming about white Cassiopeia for myself and she came home to us!

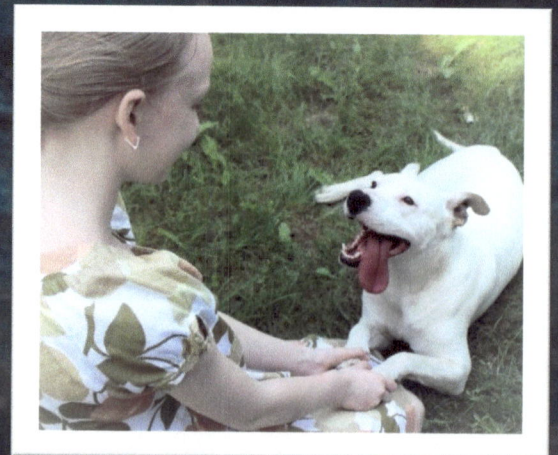

We have healed her and now we have a true faithful friend.)

I love books, traveling, music and painting, and most of all — I love my country.

"Do not be anxious about anything, but in every situation,
by prayer and petition, with thanksgiving, present your requests to God.
And the peace of God, which transcends all understanding, will guard your hearts and your minds."

(Philippians 4:6)

www.ingramcontent.com/pod-product-compliance
Lightning Source LLC
Chambersburg PA
CBHW042024090426
42811CB00016B/1734